"Emily's recipes are pure deliciousness. They are beautiful, nourishing and crave-worthy. This book is a must for anyone looking to get a creative twist on quick but healthy snacks and meals."

—Amy Lyons, author of *Fragrant Vanilla Cake*

"From their photography, to the personal touch on their writing, to each mouthwatering recipe, Emily should be so proud. Their recipes have the WOW factor every time and would get any foodie excited about eating raw food."

—Rachael Campbell, author of *Revolutionary Raw Recipes*

"Emily's recipes and photography are beautiful! They make healthy eating and compassionate living a breeze."

—Emma Potts, coconutandberries.com

"When I'm in need of inspiration, I crack open one of Emily's raw cookbooks. Their pages are absolutely filled with enticing, out-of-the-box food ideas."

—Erin Ireland, itstodiefor.ca

"Emily's beautiful recipes show their flair for creativity, passion for natural ingredients and love of harm-free living. Honest, delicious goodies that will have the world turning vegan."

—Sophie Mackenzie, wholeheartedeats.com

"Emily's book is full of brilliance and beauty! This is a must-have collection for those who crave simple wholesome foods!"

—David and Noelle McGinnis, authors of *Sacred Cookies and Elixirs*

"Emily's greatest strength is taking simple, nutritious ingredients and showcasing them in vibrant recipes that are always delicious."

—Trevor Ellestad, writer, trained yoga teacher and trained herbalist

125 BEST JUICES, SMOOTHIES

AND HEALTHY SNACKS

EASY RECIPES

for Natural Energy and Delicious,
Plant-Based Nutrition

EMILY VON EUW

author of the bestselling *Rawsome Vegan Baking*

PAGE STREET
PUBLISHING CO.

PAGE STREET
PUBLISHING CO.

First published in 2014 by
Page Street Publishing Co.
27 Congress Street, Suite 105
Salem, MA 01970
www.pagestreetpublishing.com

Distributed by Macmillan; sales in Canada by The Canadian Manda Group.

25 24 23 22 21   1 2 3 4 5

ISBN-13: 978-1-64567-458-0
ISBN-10: 1-64567-458-4

Library of Congress Control Number: 2021931971

Cover and book design by Meg Baskis for Page Street Publishing Co.
Photography by Emily von Euw

Printed and bound in the United States

CONTENTS

SWEET SMOOTHIES 133

SAVORY SMOOTHIES 193

MYLKS & MYLKSHAKES 213

ENERGY BARS & HEALTHY SNACKS 225

INTRODUCTION

Hello, hello, hello! Em von Euw here. I'm back with my new and improved edition of *100 Best Juices, Smoothies and Healthy Snacks!* This special edition includes a whole bonus chapter of 25 extra green smoothies, juices, teas and lattes. These recipes are nutrient-packed with the power of greens, but don't have that *too green* taste, if ya know what I mean. There are recipes in this new chapter for everyone in the family: from the seasoned green juice lover to kids who crave a fruity smoothie, and even folks who don't have time to get the juicer out!

Vegan-friendly living is continuing to gain popularity: More and more of us are learning—and feeling—the benefits of a plant-based approach to life. As a 10 year+ vegan myself, this couldn't make me happier. Not only is vegan living kinder to the planet and our non-human animal friends, but it's often a great choice for our physical health (but every body is different, so trust what your body needs)! While fad diets come and go, the main tenets to sustainable health and well-being are simple: eat plants, drink water, move your body, get enough sleep and laugh a lot! Smoothies, juices and plant-based snacks are an excellent method to getting enough plants in your diet every day.

This new chapter, and this entire book, showcases how you can introduce the most nutrient-dense foods on the planet into your daily meals in easy and fun ways. I think it's beautiful that these foods— fruits, veggies, nuts, seeds, beans and legumes—are not only full of beneficial components that help our bodies and minds function, but they also require substantially less resources (land and water) to produce. So go ahead, try these recipes out in your own kitchen: They might just change your life!

xo, Em

chapter 1

GREEN JUICES & SMOOTHIES

These are 25 brand new recipes, part of the revised and expanded edition of this cookbook. In this chapter you will find juices and smoothies to please every kind of palate; I offer recipes for the green drink enthusiast *and* newbie. I also offer different techniques for getting greens in your cup, because sometimes I just don't want—or have the time—to get out my juicer or blender.

Why greens? Leafy green plants are some of the most nutrient-dense, edible foods on this planet. Incorporating plenty of greens into your diet is a powerful step in the direction of holistic wellness (along with other lifestyle habits and structures like exercise, mental health care, rest and supportive relationships). Green leaves offer fiber, iron, antioxidants, vitamins A, C, K and E, folate, selenium and more! Blending green foods into smoothies, adding them to your juice, or using greens powder in lattes and teas is an easy and quick way to include these superfoods in your everyday diet. Let's go green!

SEA BUCKTHORN ORANGE JUICE WITH SPINACH AND GINGER

Sea buckthorn berries are a unique-tasting fruit. They are tart and sweet all at once and remind me of citrus . . . and candy! They offer a ton of vitamin C and thus pair well with the spinach in this recipe for maximum iron absorption.

1 cup (148 g) frozen sea buckthorn berries, thawed
1 medium orange, peeled and chopped into quarters
2 cups (60 g) spinach
1 tsp chunk ginger root

Wash, peel and chop the produce as needed. Put the berries, orange, spinach and ginger root through a juicer. Stir it all up, add some ice if desired and enjoy right away! The juice will keep for 1 to 2 days in the fridge stored in an airtight container. You can order sea buckthorn berries online or find them at your local health food store.

PEACHY SMOOTHIE WITH WHEATGRASS

Peaches, banana and wheatgrass—oh my! This is a mild and fruity smoothie to enjoy in the morning for a kick-start. I buy my wheatgrass juice in 1-ounce (28-g) frozen packs for convenience. Wheatgrass is full of iron, calcium, enzymes, magnesium, phytonutrients, amino acids, vitamins A, C, E, K and B complex, chlorophyll and even some protein. A true superfood.

1½ cups (360 ml) almond milk
1 cup (165 g) frozen peach slices
1 banana, peeled
2 tbsp (30 ml) wheatgrass juice, fresh or frozen
1 tbsp (15 ml) maple syrup
1 tsp lemon juice

In a blender, blend the almond milk, peach slices, banana, wheatgrass juice, maple syrup and lemon juice on high until smooth. Enjoy right away!

ALL THE GREENS JUICE

Sometimes you just want a hardcore green juice—this is it! If it's too intense on its own, this juice recipe can be added to fruit smoothies or other fruit juices. I crave this juice occasionally when my body wants more minerals and needs to quickly absorb more vitamins. Leafy greens are rich in vitamins C, E, A, K and B (folate), as well as iron and antioxidants. They're one of the most nutrient-dense plant foods available on earth. Leafy greens have a high fiber content, which is usually great! But when you want the nutrients of greens in an easier-to-digest format, green juice is the way to go.

1 cup (67 g) kale
1 cup (30 g) spinach
1 cup (36 g) collard greens
¼ cup (8 g) basil
4 celery stalks
½ lime, peeled
1–2 green apples, chopped into 1-inch (2.5-cm) pieces (optional)

Wash, peel and chop the produce as needed. Place the kale, spinach, collard greens, basil, celery, lime and apples (if using) in a juicer. Stir it all up, add some ice if desired and enjoy right away! The juice will keep for 1 to 2 days in the fridge stored in an airtight container.

IN A JIFFY GREEN JUICE

When I don't have access to a blender—or the motivation to use one—I make this recipe. I used to be "against" boxed juice, but there are some delicious organic ones out there that have no added sugars or anything I don't like. Those are the kind I recommend. I think it's healthiest for me to be flexible and open-minded about the foods I eat and drink. Ultimately, listening to my body is my main tool for deciding what foods work for me. When I drink this recipe, my body feels happy.

1 cup (237 ml) chilled fruit juice (I like papaya with a splash of lime, pear, apple or mango)
1 tsp spirulina powder
3 ice cubes
Pinch of stevia powder

In a jar, add the juice, spirulina, ice cubes and stevia powder. Screw on the lid and shake, shake, shake!

SUPERPOWERED MATCHA LATTE

Ahh, matcha! I am a fanatic for the stuff and have spent many years researching and exploring the history of this green tea. So I will be the first to admit: this is not a traditional recipe! But, it is tasty and full of nourishing ingredients. Matcha itself is rich in antioxidants, and I've paired it here with a vegan collagen. Consuming collagen potentially helps maintain skin and bone health. But scientific evidence supporting the benefits of collagen is currently limited. If you try a vegan collagen powder and feel a difference, great! If not, just use this recipe without the collagen for a delicious latte moment.

1 tsp ceremonial grade matcha powder, sifted
¼ cup (60 ml) hot water
½ cup (120 ml) steamed oat milk
1–2 tsp (5–10 ml) maple syrup, as desired
½ tsp vegan collagen powder
½ tsp lion's mane mushroom powder

Whisk the matcha powder and water together until foamy, then add the oat milk, maple syrup, collagen powder and mushroom powder. Whisk until smooth. Enjoy right away!

MINIMALIST GREEN JUICE

This is for those who like it simple . . . and juicy. This is a wonderfully crisp, tart juice for any time you need a pick-me-up. Lettuce in juice may sound nasty, but try it for yourself—it's actually quite subtle. Celery adds a mild, slightly salty and savory flavor. This is another recipe I crave from time to time when I want the nutrients of a giant salad but don't feel like chewing or digesting all that fiber.

1 small head green lettuce
3 celery stalks
1 lemon, peeled and chopped into quarters
1 green apple, chopped into 8 slices

Wash, peel and chop the produce as needed. In a juicer, place the lettuce, celery, lemon and apple. Stir it all up, add some ice if desired and enjoy right away! The juice will keep for 1 to 2 days in the fridge stored in airtight glassware.

LEMONGRASS AND GINGER GREEN JUICE

The flavors in this recipe all blend together with such harmony and create a fragrant, powerfully rejuvenating tonic. Lemongrass and ginger impart wonderful fresh flavors into this drink and are helpful foods for aiding digestion.

1 cup (70 g) bok choy
1 tbsp (6 g) chunk ginger root
1 orange, peeled and chopped into quarters
1 lemon, peeled and chopped into quarters
½ cup (120 ml) lemongrass tea, chilled or at room temperature

Wash, peel and chop the produce as needed. In a juicer, place the bok choy, ginger root, orange and lemon. Add the tea, mix it all up, add some ice if desired and enjoy right away! The juice will keep for 1 to 2 days in the fridge stored in an airtight container. If you're making the tea yourself, steep it for 5 minutes. But it's totally fine if it's boxed or bottled!

SIMPLE SPIRULINA DRINK

I crave this periodically, especially when my body needs more iron (spirulina has lots). It's super quick to make—no juicer needed—and if you like the unique flavor of spirulina like I do, it's yuuuummy. Sweeteners are optional!

2 cups (473 ml) chilled coconut water
1 tsp spirulina powder
1 tbsp (15 ml) lime juice
Pinch of stevia powder (optional)
1 tsp maple syrup (optional)
4 ice cubes

In a jar, add the coconut water, spirulina, lime juice, stevia (if using), maple syrup (if using) and ice. Put on the lid and shake, shake, shake! Alternatively, just stir together with a spoon. Enjoy right away, or store in the fridge for 2 to 3 days.

TUMMY-TAMING GREEN JUICE

The ingredients in this recipe are great for hydrating your body and calming tummy upsets. Cucumber contains lots of water; kale and apple contain helpful fiber; and the lemon, ginger and cayenne can help with indigestion and reduce bloating and intestinal cramping.

1 cup (120 g) cucumber, chopped in half lengthwise
1 cup (67 g) kale
1 apple, chopped into 1-inch (2.5-cm) pieces
1 lemon, peeled and chopped into quarters
1 tsp chunk ginger root
¼ tsp cayenne powder

Wash, peel and chop the produce as needed. In a juicer, place the cucumber, kale, apple, lemon and ginger root. Add the cayenne, stir it all up, add some ice if desired and enjoy right away! The juice will keep for 1 to 2 days in the fridge stored in an airtight container.

PAPAYA AND BASIL GREEN JUICE

This juice tastes like sunshine and can help soothe an upset stomach thanks to the papaya. I love serving papaya with lime: It's the way it's meant to be. Papaya, like most fruits and veggies, is great for the skin! It's also hydrating, easy to digest and full of antioxidants, which may help prevent cancer.

1 cup (30 g) spinach
¼ cup (8 g) basil
1 lime, peeled and chopped into quarters
1 cup (145 g) papaya, peeled and chopped into 1-inch (2.5-cm) pieces
Fresh basil, for garnish

Wash, peel and chop the produce as needed. In a juicer, place the spinach, basil, lime and papaya. Stir it all up, add some ice if desired and enjoy right away! The juice will keep for 1 to 2 days in the fridge stored in an airtight container. Add a sprig of basil, if desired.

FRUITY GINGER GREEN JUICE

Consuming leafy greens and calming foods like ginger, mint and lemon can have a great effect on improving digestion. This is one big reason I like smoothies and juice—they make it easy to get in all my fruits and veggies, fiber and antioxidants.

1 apple, chopped into 1-inch (2.5-cm) pieces
1 cup (151 g) green grapes
¼ cup (8 g) mint
½ lemon, peeled
1 tsp chunk ginger root
½ cup (120 ml) nettle tea, chilled or at room temperature

Wash, peel and chop the produce as needed. In a juicer, place the apple, grapes, mint, lemon and ginger root. Mix the juice with the tea, add some ice if desired and enjoy right away! The juice will keep for 1 to 2 days in the fridge stored in an airtight container.

HONEYDEW AND BASIL JUICE

This is the essence of summer for me and one of my favorite recipes in this chapter. Fresh melons at the farmers' market and basil from the garden boxes on the balcony—*ahh*! You can almost see the sunshine in the glass when you pour this juice.

2 cups (320 g) honeydew, chopped into 1-inch (2.5-cm) pieces
¼ cup (8 g) basil leaves
1 lime, peeled and chopped into quarters

Wash, peel and chop the produce as needed. In a juicer, place the honeydew, basil and lime. Stir it all up, add some ice if desired and enjoy right away! The juice will keep for 1 to 2 days in the fridge stored in an airtight container.

CITRUS-CENTRIC GREEN JUICE

I love citrus: It's tangy, sweet, acidic and vibrant all at once. Citrus brightens up any recipe—sweet or savory—and is full of vitamin C and other antioxidants to keep your body happy. There are so many more citrus fruits beyond oranges and lemons! Pomelos and tangelos are two of my favorites.

P.S. This recipe makes a lot of juice, so I recommend making it for a party or get-together where it can be shared fresh.

1 grapefruit, peeled and chopped into 1-inch (2.5-cm) pieces
½ pomelo, peeled and chopped into 1-inch (2.5-cm) pieces
2 tangelos, peeled and chopped into quarters
1 lemon, peeled and chopped into quarters
1 cup (36 g) rainbow chard

Wash, peel and chop the produce as needed. In a juicer, place the grapefruit, pomelo, tangelos, lemon and rainbow chard. Because of all the citrus rind in this recipe, you may wish to strain the juice before drinking. Up to you! Add some ice if desired and enjoy right away! The juice will keep for 1 to 2 days in the fridge stored in an airtight container.

GREEN SMOOTHIE WITH APPLE AND KALE JUICE

This is one of my all-time favorite recipes. First, we juice apple, kale and ginger, and then we blend it with frozen banana for a creamy, dreamy, fruit bevvy. Yes, it's an extra step, but it's worth it! This recipe tastes like a green juice mylkshake (does that only sound good to me or are there other green juice freaks out there!?). If you'd like it creamier and thicker, use two bananas or even some coconut milk!

1 apple, chopped into 1-inch (2.5-cm) pieces
2 cups (134 g) kale
1 tsp chunk ginger root
1–2 frozen bananas, as desired

Wash, peel and chop the produce as needed. Put the apple, kale and ginger through a juicer. Then add the juice to a blender with the banana. Blend until smooth. Add some ice if desired and enjoy right away!

FRUITY GREEN JUICE WITH PEAR AND GRAPE

This one's for the folks who want greens but don't love the taste of "green juice." The spinach is nice and mild, and you can hardly taste the kale because the grapes, pear and apple offer lots of delicious, natural sweetness. Fruit juice straight from the juicer is in a league of its own as far as flavor goes; plus, juicing fruit yourself provides way more nutrients than the stuff that's been sitting on the shelf for a while.

1 green apple, chopped into 1-inch (2.5-cm) pieces
1 Anjou pear, chopped into quarters
1 cup (151 g) green grapes
2 cups (60 g) spinach
1 cup (67 g) kale
¼ cup (8 g) mint
½ lime, peeled

Wash, peel and chop the produce as needed. In a juicer, place the apple, pear, grapes, spinach, kale, mint and lime. Stir it all up, add some ice if desired and enjoy right away! The juice will keep for 1 to 2 days in the fridge stored in an airtight container.

SAVORY VEGGIE JUICE

This juice is perfect for when you want green juice without too much sweetness. The color on this one is not so vibrant, but the flavor is delicious when you're in the right mood! I personally don't love the flavor of bell peppers, but they are super rich in vitamin C, so I sneak them into drinks and meals when I can.

½ cup (35 g) cabbage, chopped into 1-inch (2.5-cm) pieces
½ cup (46 g) broccoli, chopped into 1-inch (2.5-cm) pieces
6 celery stalks
½ cup (59 g) cucumber
1 green bell pepper, chopped into quarters
1 lemon, peeled and chopped into quarters
1 tsp chunk ginger root
1 apple, chopped into 1-inch (2.5-cm) pieces (optional)

Wash, peel and chop the produce as needed. In a juicer, place the cabbage, broccoli, celery, cucumber, bell pepper, lemon, ginger root and apple (if using). Stir it all up, add some ice if desired and enjoy right away! The juice will keep for 1 to 2 days in the fridge stored in an airtight container.

ZINGY GREEN JUICE

Thanks to the lettuce and bell pepper, this is milder green juice in terms of bitterness. But I like tart juice sometimes, so we are adding green apple and lemon for that puckered lip experience. I loooove adding lettuce to juices because it tastes and feels so hydrating.

5 cups (150 g) lettuce
1 green bell pepper, chopped into quarters
1 green apple, chopped into 1-inch (2.5-cm) pieces
1 lemon, peeled and chopped into quarters

Wash, peel and chop the produce as needed. In a juicer, place the lettuce, bell pepper, apple and lemon. Stir it all up, add some ice if desired and enjoy right away! The juice will keep for 1 to 2 days in the fridge stored in airtight glassware.

GOOD MORNING MORINGA DRINK

This simple, quick recipe is kind on your tummy. Plus, it offers a gentle wake-up for your body in the morning (though you can make it any time). Moringa oleifera is a plant that has been used in South Asia and Africa for millennia, especially in Indian Ayurvedic medicine. The tree has been called The Miracle Tree, The Wonder Tree and The Divine Tree because of its many uses and benefits. Moringa is highly nutritious, offering vitamins A, B and C, iron, magnesium and protein!

1½ cups (360 ml) hot water
½ tsp moringa powder
½–1 tsp lime juice, as desired
½ tsp fresh grated ginger root
1 tsp maple syrup

Combine the water, moringa powder, lime juice, ginger root and maple syrup. Stir together all the ingredients until smooth. Let sit for a minute to let the ginger infuse. Strain through a fine sieve to remove the grated ginger. Drink immediately!

TROPICAL FRUIT SMOOTHIE WITH GREENS

I love tropical fruits. I live in the Pacific Northwest where there are delicious apples and stone fruits aplenty, but I still have a deep love for magical treats like papaya and mango. Here we are blending them with greens for a super nutrient-dense, sweet smoothie. This is one of my favorite recipes in the book!

1 cup (237 ml) coconut water (for a juicy smoothie) or coconut milk (for a creamy smoothie)
½ cup (72 g) papaya, chopped into 1-inch (2.5-cm) pieces
½ cup (83 g) frozen mango, chopped into 1-inch (2.5-cm) pieces
½ cup (83 g) frozen pineapple, chopped into 1-inch (2.5-cm) pieces
1 tbsp (15 ml) lime juice
¼ tsp spirulina powder
¼ tsp wheatgrass powder
¼ tsp chlorella powder
¼ tsp moringa powder
Pinch of stevia powder (optional)

Wash, peel and chop the produce as needed. In a blender, place the coconut water or milk, papaya, mango, pineapple and lime juice. Then add the spirulina, wheatgrass, chlorella, moringa and stevia (if using) powders. Blend until smooth. Stop blending as soon as you don't see chunks of fruit anymore, otherwise the mango will get gelatinous. Add an ice cube or two if desired. Enjoy right away!

FENNEL GINGER SMOOTHIE FOR PMS

Fennel and ginger are very effective at relieving menstrual pain. Here's an easy and delicious way to get them both in a green drink. Plus, we add raspberry leaf tea for cramp relief! I honestly feel the calming effects of this drink right away. Even if you don't have the energy to make this when you're experiencing PMS, try to add a little ginger powder and fennel into your day!

1 cup (237 ml) almond milk
1 green apple, chopped into quarters (or banana for a creamier smoothie)
1 cup (30 g) swiss chard
½ cup (83 g) frozen mango chunks
¼ tsp ginger powder
⅛ tsp fennel seeds
Pinch of stevia powder
½ cup (120 ml) raspberry leaf tea, chilled or at room temperature (optional)

Wash, peel and chop the produce as needed. In a blender, place the almond milk, apple, swiss chard, mango, ginger powder, fennel seeds and stevia. Blend until smooth. Stop blending as soon as you don't see chunks of fruit anymore, otherwise the mango will get gelatinous. Add the tea, if using. Add an ice cube or two, if desired. Enjoy right away!

ADAPTOGENIC VANILLA MATCHA SMOOTHIE

A delicious green tea smoothie full of brain foods, great for having with breakfast or as a morning snack. Green tea, originating in China, has been enjoyed for millennia. Matcha and the matcha ceremony (aka chanoyu) have a rich and long history in Japanese culture. I am sensitive to caffeine (which matcha contains because it's a type of green tea) so I am cautious not to have this from the afternoon onward. I recommend adding ice for an iced matcha latte!

1 cup (237 ml) vanilla oat milk
1 tsp ceremonial grade matcha
1–2 tsp (5–10 ml) maple syrup
½ tsp wheatgrass powder
½ tsp lion's mane mushroom powder (or other mushroom powder, like chaga or reishi)

Blend the milk, matcha, maple syrup, wheatgrass and lion's mane powders and ice cubes (if using) in a blender until smooth. Remember to add the sweetener to taste. Enjoy right away! Add two or three ice cubes, if desired.

GREEN SMOOTHIE FOR GLOWY SKIN

This smoothie is great for the skin . . . and the whole self! Which makes sense, since the body, mind and spirit are really one sweet organism. Spinach offers iron and other micronutrients, banana is rich in potassium, rice milk contains manganese and selenium and cucumber is hydrating. Feel free to add some collagen if you find it works for you (the science on consuming collagen is still out, but some people swear by it—so just go with what feels right for you).

1 cup (30 g) spinach
1 frozen banana
1 cup (237 ml) rice milk
¼ cup (30 g) cucumber, chopped into 1-inch (2.5-cm) pieces
1 tsp maple syrup
1 tsp vegan collagen powder (optional)

Wash, peel and chop the produce as needed. In a blender, add the spinach, banana, milk, cucumber, maple syrup and collagen (if using). Blend until smooth. Add an ice cube or two, if desired. Enjoy right away!

ALL THE GOODS
GREEN SMOOTHIE

This smoothie has a lot going on. We are adding a bunch of different veggies, fruits and hemp seeds. This is a great recipe to have with, or for, breakfast or as a filling drink during the day. I recommend sharing this with someone, because it makes a lot of smoothie!

1 cup (237 ml) almond milk
1 green apple, chopped into 1-inch (2.5-cm) pieces
½ cup (90 g) frozen peach slices
½ frozen banana
2 ice cubes
½ yellow bell pepper, chopped into 1-inch (2.5-cm) pieces
½ cup (15 g) spinach
½ cup (15 g) swiss chard
1 tsp lemon juice
2 tbsp (18 g) hemp seeds
1–2 pitted medjool dates, as desired

Wash, peel and chop the produce as needed. In a blender, put the milk, apple, peaches, banana, ice cubes, bell pepper, spinach, swiss chard, lemon juice, hemp seeds and dates. Blend until smooth. Add an ice cube or two, if desired. Enjoy right away!

GINGER CARROT JUICE WITH THE GREENS

A simple but delicious recipe; it is sweet with a bit of tanginess from the pineapple and ginger. Carrot greens are super nutritious, so we are adding them along with the carrots. You can do the same with beets. Don't toss that good stuff!

3 medium carrots with greens
½ cup (83 g) pineapple, chopped into 1-inch (2.5-cm) pieces
½ tsp chunk ginger root
½ lemon, peeled

Wash, peel and chop the produce as needed. In a blender, place the carrots, pineapple, ginger root and lemon. Blend until smooth. Add an ice cube or two, if desired. Enjoy right away!

SPIRULINA VANILLA MYLKSHAKE

What is the tastiest way to get your daily dose of greens? In a mylkshake, of course! The secret to the creaminess of this recipe is the full-fat coconut milk. I find it too rich on its own, so we add a little rice milk to balance it out. I like adding lemon or lime to spirulina recipes because it brightens up the flavor profile.

Tip: If you don't have frozen bananas on hand, just add some ice cubes and a little less milk.

2 frozen bananas, chopped into 1-inch (2.5-cm) pieces
¼ cup (60 ml) full-fat coconut milk
½ cup (120 ml) rice milk
1 tbsp (15 ml) maple syrup
½ tsp vanilla extract
1 tsp spirulina powder
½ tsp lemon juice

In a blender, add the bananas, coconut and rice milks, maple syrup, vanilla, spirulina and lemon juice and blend on high speed. It might take a minute for the bananas to get blended. Be patient; they will suddenly become the consistency of a dreamy mylkshake. Enjoy right away!

chapter 2

SWEET JUICES

Everybody loves fruit juice. It's sweet, fresh as well as refreshing and great for you! So with that logic, I think this will probably be a very popular chapter. You can juice almost any fruit (except for bananas and avocados) into an incredibly delicious elixir of health and glowing color. A lot of my sweet juice recipes also include dark leafy greens and non-sweet fruits (think cucumbers, bell peppers and lemons), not only to balance out the sweetness but also to add extra nutrition. For example, kale is mega-good for your bod and if I can sneak it in with some pineapple, I'm gonna.

Keep in mind that when you juice plants, you're taking out the fiber. Fiber slows down digestion, assimilation and absorption so when you get rid of it, you speed all that stuff up. This is the main benefit to making and drinking juice, but for those of us with sensitive blood sugar levels, it can be an issue because the sugars in the juice are almost instantly absorbed. Personally, this is not a problem for me—I can drink a huge glass of pure watermelon juice and be begging for more—but every body is different so I thought it'd be wise to mention this. Fortunately, most of my sweet juice recipes aren't really super sweet anyway, and this is the only chapter you need to be concerned about this with.

Again, as a reminder, do not juice seeds as they can be toxic!

LIME AND APPLE AURA

Your body will love you for drinking this, and it will show both inside and out. Apples are great for the skin, and limes are terrific for your digestive system. I think this recipe is reminiscent of "limeade."

2 green apples
2 limes
1 cucumber

Wash, peel and chop the produce as needed, removing any seeds from the fruit. Put everything through your juicer, sip, get the glow.

LUSCIOUS LIVER TONIC

All the ingredients in this juice help to increase liver function and keep "everything moving." This is a great detox recipe, or the perfect wake-me-up in the morning!

8 radishes
2 green apples
2 beets
4 carrots
1 tbsp (15 g) ginger

Wash, peel and chop the produce as needed, removing any seeds from the fruit. Put everything through a juicer and enjoy.

SWEET SUNSHINE

Ginger is an excellent blood cleanser, and pineapple and lemon work to alkalize your stomach, creating a happy habitat for digestion (a healthy gut = a healthy you). Finally, bell peppers carry a surprisingly high amount of vitamin C. All the ingredients combined create a vibrant, glowing yellow juice that will impress even the most skeptical folks.

1 yellow bell pepper
1 tbsp (15 g) ginger
1 lemon
2 cups (330 g) pineapple
3 red apples

Wash, peel and chop the produce as needed, removing any seeds from the fruit. Put through your juicer and enjoy in the sun!

CITRUS SITUATION

So. Much. Citrus. Hopefully you were spared from the brain-numbing effects of a reality TV show called *Jersey Shore*, but sadly I was not, and I think my subconscious had something to do with naming this one. "We've got a sitch!"

3 grapefruits
2 lemons
2 green apples
3 oranges

Wash, peel and chop the produce as needed, removing any seeds from the fruit. Then juuuuuice! Put all the ingredients through your juicer, and enjoy right away!

KUMQUATS
BE KIND

Wow! I had never had kumquats before making this juice, and I was blown away by their unique and fresh flavor! Citrusy, sweet and super juicy—they are like little explosions of sunshine in your mouth. Try to buy them organic! Note: You can leave the kumquats whole, no need to peel 'em.

2 cups (290 g) kumquats
1 orange bell pepper
2 oranges
2 red apples
1 cucumber

Wash, peel and chop the produce as needed, removing any seeds from the fruit. Then throw it all in the juicer!

KALE AND CARROT KARMA

Good vibes abound! Carrots are full of feel-good vitamins, and their color alone is enough to cheer me up. Kale is one the most nutrient-dense foods on this planet, and the most efficient way to absorb those nutrients is by juicing the leaves. This is a great morning juice to wake up your body and mind! I love sipping it after practicing yoga.

6 carrots
2 green apples
1 clove garlic
5 cups (335 g) kale
1 cucumber

Wash, peel and chop the produce as needed, removing any seeds from the fruit. Put everything through your juicer, then feel the karma waves.

BUDDHA-FUL BEETS

Earthliness in abundance! I absolutely adore beet juice. Its subtle sweetness and earthy tones create a wonderful drink and when paired with herbs (as in this recipe), it can't be beet! Whoops—I meant beat . . . no, I didn't.

3 beets
1 cup (16 g) cilantro
1 red apple
1 lime

Wash, peel and chop the produce as needed, removing any seeds from the fruit. Put everything through your juicer, going slowly with the beets because they're very dense.

SO FRESH, SO CLEAN

This is a super hydrating drink, full of amazingly juicy and flavorful ingredients: cucumber, watermelon and pineapple. Add some coconut water and/or a pinch of salt (for electrolytes) and this is the perfect thing to sip during a workout! The fresh mint leaves round off the drink and make for a delicious, refreshing elixir. P.S. The name of this recipe is inspired by the *funkalicious* Outkast track. Give it a listen.

½ watermelon
1 cucumber
2 cups (330 g) pineapple
1 cup (25 g) mint leaves
1 cup (5 g) ice cubes

Wash, peel and chop the produce as needed, removing any seeds from the fruit. Juice the watermelon, cucumber and pineapple. Serve with ice and mint leaves. *Ahhh.*

PEPPERMINT PICK ME UP

Refreshing, sweet and sure to help open your eyes in the morning, this juice is also great for calming an upset tummy, thanks to the ginger and mint.

1 cucumber
2 green apples
1 cup (25 g) mint leaves
1 tbsp (15 g) ginger

Wash, peel and chop the produce as needed, removing any seeds from the fruit. Put them all through your juicer and get your morning started right!

HONEY-TO-DEW LIST

My parents and I thought we were so clever when we came up with the name for this one. Get it? To-do list? Honey-to-dew list? Honeydew melon? Okay—clever or lame, this recipe tastes great. It's subtly sweet, and the lime brings on a lot of fresh flavor. Sip it in the summer!

1 honeydew melon
2 grapefruits
1 lime

Wash, peel and chop the produce as needed, removing any seeds from the fruit. Then put through your juicer and enjoy!

FENNEL CITRUS SUSTENANCE

The myriad of glimmering citrus fruits as well as the fennel in this recipe all come together to create a juice that has the perfect balance of sweet and tart; it's now one of my favorite juices. Blood oranges are one of the most gorgeous fruits I have ever seen!

2 blood oranges
2 cups (175 g) fennel
1 grapefruit
1 lime
2 oranges

Wash, peel and chop the produce as needed, removing any seeds from the fruit. Try to keep some pith on the oranges—it's got lots of nutrients! Put all the ingredients through your juicer, and enjoy right away!

SEXY SATISFYING WATERMELON JUICE WITH PEPPERMINT

If "food porn" is a legitimate term, can "juice porn" be a thing, too? I mean, look at this photo.

1 watermelon
¼ cup (6 g) peppermint leaves
3 ice cubes

Chop up the watermelon and then blend it into juice—it will liquify almost immediately. I blended up my watermelon in two batches because it was huge. Strain your juice and then pour it over the mint leaves and ice. Slurp! So hydrating and sweet!

POWER GREENS

An all-around great green juice recipe that will give ya everything you need in one glass.

4 cups (270 g) kale
1 cup (16 g) cilantro
1 cucumber
1 tbsp (15 g) ginger
1 clove garlic
1 green apple
1 lemon

Wash, peel and chop the produce as needed, removing any seeds from the fruit. Put through your juicer and savor the nourishment that comes out.

EVERYDAY JUICE

This is my mom's go-to juice every morning and an excellent way to start your day.

1 grapefruit
2 green apples
2 carrots
1 cucumber
1 tbsp (15 g) ginger
1 orange

Wash, peel and chop the produce as needed, removing any seeds from the fruit. Then put it all through your juicer and enjoy.

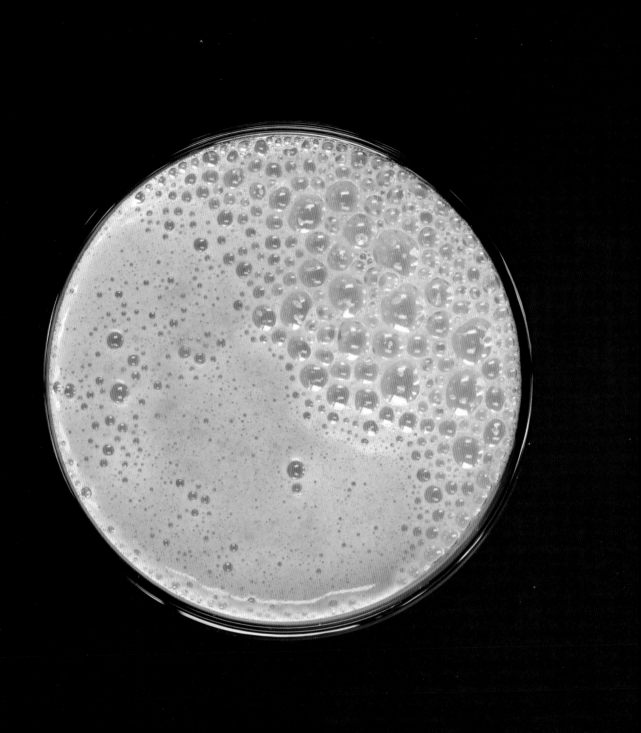

CARROT APPLE LIME

This one might make ya pucker your lips because of the tartness of the lime—but I love it.

6 carrots
2 red apples
2 limes

Wash, peel and chop the produce as needed, removing any seeds from the fruit. Put it all through the juicer and enjoy!

WATERMELON WAKE ME UP

One of the most refreshing and sexy drinks in this book. No joke.

½ watermelon
1 lime
1 cucumber

Wash, peel and chop the produce as needed, removing any seeds from the fruit. Juice it up! Put all the ingredients through your juicer, and enjoy right away!

HERB HAPPINESS

This one tastes pretty unusual . . . but I think it tastes weird in a good way. I hope
that makes sense.

1 cup (16 g) mint leaves
1 cup (16 g) cilantro
1 green apple
1 orange

Wash, peel and chop the produce as needed, removing any seeds from the fruit. Put all the
ingredients through your juicer, and enjoy right away! Savor the odd flavor.

STRAWBERRY LEMONADE

Perfect for summer. Enjoy a tall glass of health and deliciousness all at once.

2 cups (288 g) strawberries
1 lemon
1 pineapple
½ cup (2.5 g) ice

Wash, peel and chop the produce as needed, removing any seeds from the fruit. Then juice everything, serve with ice and enjoy.

LETTUCE TURNIP THE BEET

I can't take credit for the punny title. It's been going around the Internet for a while, making people from all walks of life groan at the lame humor plants provide.

2 beets
1 head lettuce
3 turnips
3 carrots
2 green apples

Wash, peel and chop the produce as needed, removing any seeds from the fruit. Put all the ingredients through your juicer, and enjoy right away!

chapter 3

SAVORY JUICES

Here's the deal: Savory juices are flipping amazing (that was more my opinion than a deal . . . but *shh*). Maybe when I say juice, you just think I mean sweet fruit juices. Nope. Vegetables juice wonderfully into flavorful fountains of all colors and potencies. If you're looking to lose weight, these savory veggie juices are your new best friend. I'm talkin' BFFs here. Why is this? Vegetables are extremely low in calories, high in water content and incredibly nutrient dense. That means you can eat—or drink—them to your heart's content and effortlessly find your natural healthy weight. Drink vegetable juice—especially with dark leafy greens—every day for a long life and a beautiful figure.

MEAN, GREEN AND CLEAN

This is a great juice to start your day with. It includes a bunch of water-rich ingredients as well as powerful disease fighters (if it's dark green and leafy, it's probably amazing for you).

2 cups (135 g) kale
2 green apples
1 lime
3 celery stalks
1 cup (60 g) parsley
1 clove garlic
1 green bell pepper
1 cucumber

Wash, peel and chop the produce as needed, removing any seeds from the fruit. Put everything through your juicer, alternating between greens and juicy fruits to keep the juicer lubricated. Sip up the nutrition with a smile!

V8^2

Why is it squared? Because this recipe packs twice the nutritional punch! I am aware that squaring something does not really mean multiplying it by two, but let's just suspend mathematical reality for a second so we can get excited about this juice; it's got <u>ALL</u> the good things.

3 tomatoes
1 lemon
1 clove garlic
1 tbsp (15 g) ginger
1 green apple
1 orange
1 grapefruit
1 cucumber
3 carrots
2 cups (32 g) cilantro
1 cup (16 g) peppermint
2 cups (134 g) kale
1 bell pepper
2 golden beets
3 celery stalks
3 pineapple slices

Wash, peel and chop the produce as needed, removing any seeds from the fruit. Juuuuuuice it all up.

KALE CRAVER

The first time I made this recipe and took a sip I immediately exclaimed, "You are what I have been craving!" Hence the name of the drink. Get energized, nourished and hydrated all in one glorious glass. That's what I'm talkin' 'bout.

2 green apples
3 cups (201 g) kale
6 celery stalks
1 cucumber
1 clove garlic
1 tbsp (15 g) ginger
1 lemon

Wash, peel and chop the produce as needed, removing any seeds from the fruit. Put everything through your juicer and drink up the goodness.

TOMATO GARLIC GREATNESS

I was gonna call this one "power to the prostate" because tomatoes are excellent for prostate health—but I didn't want to exclude those of us without one, either! Tomatoes are full of nutrients that are beneficial for everyone.

2 cloves garlic
5 tomatoes
3 carrots
1 cucumber

Wash, peel and chop the produce as needed. If you're using an organic cucumber, you can leave the skin on! Put all the ingredients through your juicer, and enjoy right away! Feel the power.

JICAMA SWEETHEART

The name is a little deceiving because this recipe isn't actually all that sweet in flavor or in subtlety! The onions, garlic and ginger make for one powerful potion and I promise you will be feeling the detoxification and blood-cleansing effects as soon as you start sipping this. Seriously, drink it slowly.

4 cups (385 g) jicama
¼ cup (38 g) onion
1 clove garlic
1 tbsp (15 g) ginger
1 lemon
1–2 green apples (optional)

Wash, peel and chop the produce as needed. Remove the seeds from the apple, if you're adding one. Put everything through a juicer. If it's too strong for you, add an apple or two.

VELVET VIBRATIONS

If you listen to Bootsy Collins, then you'll know this recipe's name is inspired by "Love Vibrations," or I guess you could think of the better known Beach Boys hit, "Good Vibrations." But also, when I think of velvet I think of smoothness, and the ingredients in this juice are all easy on the tummy and useful for improved digestion—keeping things running smoothly.

4 beets
6 small carrots
1 clove garlic
1 cucumber
1 bell pepper
1 cup (16 g) peppermint leaves
2 tomatoes
¼ cup (38 g) onion
3 small zucchini

Wash, peel and chop the produce as needed, removing any seeds from the fruit, then put through your juicer. This one is really nice strained.

VIRUS VIGILANTE

You can call this one Flu Fighter if ya want, but I feel like every juice bar has a drink called that, and I'm trying to be original. Gimme a break, okay? The important thing is that this juice is one potent tonic! Touting over 1,200 percent of your daily required vitamin C (thanks to the camu camu powder), it will probably kick any sickness you might feel coming on. Plus, it's delicious.

1 lemon
1 clove garlic
1 tbsp (15 g) ginger
1 green apple
1 tbsp (7 g) camu camu powder

Wash, peel and chop the produce as needed, removing any seeds from the fruit, then put it all through your juicer. Throw the juice in a blender with the camu camu powder and blend for just a sec until it is incorporated. Chug!

CARROT GINGER SIPPER

Sip it slow, because the ginger is potent!

3 carrots
1 tbsp (15 g) ginger
1 red apple
1 lemon

Wash, peel and chop the produce as needed, removing any seeds from the fruit. Put everything through your juicer and enjoy!

LETTUCE AND FENNEL FENG SHUI

This recipe is great for settling upset stomachs or easing digestion, thanks to the fennel. The other ingredients all help with blood flow and detoxification. Cheers to a balanced life full of chi (vital universal energy)!

6 cups (330 g) lettuce
1 cucumber
1 lime
1 cup (87.5 g) fennel
1 green apple

Wash, peel and chop the produce as needed, removing any seeds from the fruit. Put it all through the juicer and sip up the good vibes.

SPRING CLEANER

Supa fresh! Supa good! The perfect way to start your morning and keep your body happy, healthy, hydrated and glowing.

1 green apple
5 cups (650 g) kale
1 lemon
1 cucumber

Wash, peel and chop the produce as needed, removing any seeds from the fruit. Throw through your juicer and enjoy!

SALSA SEDUCTION

My friend from Mexico tells me that this is basically pico de gallo, minus the super spicy serrano pepper. I can dig it . . . I mean, drink it!

1 clove garlic
1 cup (180 g) tomatoes
1 cup (16 g) cilantro
1 lime
1 yellow bell pepper
½ cucumber
¼ cup (62 g) onion (optional)
¼ tsp ground cumin

Wash, peel and chop the produce as needed. Remember to remove the seeds from the bell pepper and then put it all through the juicer (except the cumin). Mix the cumin into the juice and enjoy!

RADICAL ROOTZ

Root veggies are super great for you because they take in all the nutrients in the soil they are growing in, and they have an amazing earthy flavor that I am deeply in love with. Besides, the color of this juice is a work of art in itself.

3 beets
6 carrots
1 tbsp (15 g) ginger
1 celeriac root

Wash, peel and chop the produce as needed. Throw it all through the juicer and enjoy!

KIDNEY CONSCIOUS

The main ingredient in this recipe is celeriac (or celery root), which is known to play a role in detoxification and stimulating kidney function. Not surprisingly, the flavor is similar to celery: refreshing and light. I like to pair it with citrus.

1 celeriac root
1 grapefruit

Wash, peel and chop the produce as needed, removing any seeds from the fruit. Put all the ingredients through your juicer, and enjoy right away!

SUNNY SIDE UP

The special ingredient in this recipe is sunchokes (often called Jerusalem artichokes). Similar to ginger root in appearance, sunchokes have a delicious flavor and are great for the body; they have three times more iron than broccoli and have been shown to boost immune system function.

3 sunchokes
1 green apple
1 tbsp (15 g) ginger

Wash, peel and chop the produce as needed, removing any seeds from the fruit. Put all the ingredients through your juicer, and enjoy right away!

ENERGIZER BUNNY

One of my first animal companions, a rabbit whom I named Cottontail, was always begging me to feed her crunchy carrots and juicy celery. Munching on them all day was her idea of paradise. She had great instincts! Both of these foods are terrific for your entire body, as well as super hydrating. I'm saving myself the munching step and throwing them right through the juicer for faster nutrient absorption. Let's bounce.

5 celery stalks
5 large carrots

Wash, peel and chop the carrots and celery as needed, then put them through your juicer, alternating between the two and going slowly (carrots can be tough to juice sometimes). Enjoy!

SAVORY BEETS

I've said it before and I will say it again: I love the earthy flavor of beets. Those tones go great with garlic and ginger, and that is pretty much what this juice is. It's a nice one for mid-morning, in my humble opinion.

2 beets
1 tbsp (15 g) ginger
1 clove garlic
2 carrots

Wash, peel and chop the produce as needed. Put everything through your juicer, alternating the beets with the other ingredients, and enjoy!

ONE LOVE LETTUCE

This recipe is pretty green, so I recommend getting used to less-sweet juices before making it so you don't think it's too bitter to drink. Having said that, once you get accustomed—it is delicious!

2 heads lettuce
1 cucumber
5 celery stalks
1 lemon
1 green apple

Wash, peel and chop the produce as needed, removing any seeds from the fruit. Put all the ingredients through your juicer, and enjoy right away!

BET YOUR BORSCHT

Pretty unique flavors going on in this one. . . .

3 beets
½ head red cabbage
1 bunch dill
1 clove garlic
1 red apple

Wash, peel and chop the produce as needed, removing any seeds from the fruit. Juice it up. Drink it down.

WHEATGRASS SHOTS

Because wheatgrass is so potent and powerful, you don't need much! Drink these on an empty stomach to get the most benefits. You can buy wheatgrass trays at some health food stores, or grow your own for cheap! Just search it on the Internet to learn how. You also need a high-quality juicer to successfully juice wheatgrass—check out the brands I recommend on page 248.

1 (21" x 11" x 2" [53 x 28 x 5-cm]) tray wheatgrass

Cut the grass near the root, rinse it off and then put through your juicer . . . time for shots!

chapter 4

SWEET SMOOTHIES

Delicious any time of day (especially for breakfast), the smoothie recipes in this chapter are perfect for providing quickly absorbed energy and fantastic flavor. Sweet fruits are a key to long-term health and wellness; they contain incredible amounts of antioxidants that have been proven to prevent and fight cancer and a plethora of other chronic diseases and illnesses. They are also very high in water content (making them super hydrating) and essential vitamins, minerals and nutrients. The majority of my diet is made up of sweet fruits; they are the ideal food for humans because of the balance of their water content, calorie count, nutritional density and amount of fiber. There are no bad fruits!

If you have trouble getting all of your 5 to 10 recommended servings of fruit on a daily basis, then this is the chapter for you. In one colorful and tasty glass, you can sip up all that goodness in minutes and get on with the day. Having said that, 5 to 10 fruits a day is still on the low side in my opinion. Try to get in as many fruits and vegetables as possible every day: the more, the better. These smoothies are full of juicy, sweet fruits, making them really easy for all to enjoy. Trying to get your kids to eat healthier? Hand them a Mint Cacao Kiss (page 166) and they'll be pleading for seconds.

All of these would be great for post-workout nutrition because they are full of good carbs that your body requires after cardiovascular exercise. If you're working out for a longer period of time and using weights, simply throw in a scoop of your favorite plant-based protein powder (I love Vega), and your muscles will thank you.

THE BASIC GREEN

This could also be called "The Essential Smoothie" because it's just that. It is infinitely adaptable so you can change it up every day while still following the same fundamental recipe. Instead of spinach, use any dark leafy greens; instead of strawberries, use any frozen fruit; and instead of mylk, use any liquid (like water or fresh juice)! I drink this every morning after I exercise; it is what my body craves. Have fun! Get sexy!

2 bananas
3 cups (675 g) spinach
1 cup (150 g) frozen strawberries
2 cups (473 ml) basic mylk (page 214)

Blend until smooth . . . *ahh*. Big smile.

APPLE CINNAMON DELIGHT

This tastes like apple pie in a mug. Enough said? Yep.

3 large apples, seeds removed
3 bananas
2 tsp (5 g) cinnamon
1 tsp nutmeg
1–2 cups (237–473 ml) spiced mylk (page 217)

Blend all the ingredients together until smooth and creamy, adding spices as desired. Sprinkle some cinnamon on top and enjoy.

GRAPEFRUIT MANGO IMMUNE BOOSTER

Don't want to get a cold? Drink this. All the ingredients are very high in vitamin C, which acts as a natural antihistamine and has been proven to help prevent colds as well as shorten their duration. It is also high in antioxidants that fight everything from cancer to cataracts to high blood pressure. If you like the flavor of grapefruit, you'll love this one.

1 grapefruit
1 cup (151 g) frozen mango
1 cup (165 g) pineapple
1 cup (237 ml) water

Slice all the rind off the grapefruit. Blend all ingredients together until smooth and orange-pinkish. Gulp down the goodness.

GINGER PEPPERMINT LIVER CLEANSER

Peppermint leaves help your liver by increasing bile flow while breaking down fats and lowering bad cholesterol. Ginger has been proven to prevent diseases associated with the liver as well as cleanse the blood. Health benefits aside, the flavors combine with tropical fruits to make one deliciously fresh drink. Have this one in the morning to start your day off right.

1 cup (24 g) packed mint leaves
2 bananas
4 ice cubes
1 tbsp (15 g) ginger
1 cup (165 g) pineapple
1–3 cups (237–710 ml) water

Blend all ingredients until smooth and green, making sure there aren't any fibers from the ginger left unblended . . . they get in your teeth.

BERRY BERRY BEAR HUG

They might look ferocious, but normally a bear's idea of a perfect day is nibbling on berries in the quiet forest; I can relate. This smoothie is bursting with blueberries and strawberries, as well as some walnuts, bananas and fresh vanilla bean. Share the love!

2 cups (310 g) frozen blueberries
2 cups (298 g) frozen strawberries
2 bananas
1 cup (237 ml) water
¼ cup (29 g) walnuts
½ vanilla bean

Blend it up until smooth and frosty. Drink.

BANANA SPINACH ALMOND DREAM

If you don't want to eat a giant bag of spinach every day—but know you should be consuming more greens—try this recipe out. The fresh almond milk and bananas balance out the spinach and create a creamy, sweet drink that also counts as a giant salad!

2 bananas
1 cup (165 g) frozen pineapple
2 cups (473 ml) basic mylk (page 214)
4 cups (120 g) spinach
1 orange

Remove the seeds from the orange. Blend up everything until smooth and evenly colored (it'll be a vibrant green). Slurp!

SPIRULINA POWER

I love drinking this smoothie right after a workout to nourish my muscles. Spirulina (green algae) is packed with protein, vitamin B2, copper and iron: All of these work to rebuild muscle tissue and give you energy for the rest of the day! It helps rid heavy metals and other bodily waste from the system. Don't be intimidated by the color of spirulina powder . . . that dark green means it's full of chlorophyll (an amazing blood cleanser and cancer-fighting molecule).

2 oranges
1 cup (165 g) pineapple
2 bananas
5 ice cubes
1 tbsp (1 g) spirulina powder

Blend until smooth. Enjoy.

BERRY CITRUS BLITZ

I recommend using a berry medley in this recipe for a larger variety of benefits and flavors. Although I believe all plants were created equal . . . blueberries are shamelessly my favorite. I wait all year for our bushes to blossom, and my diet in the summer ends up being largely blueberries. Berries have been praised for ages for their amazing antioxidant content (they're basically cancer-fighting super-heroes) as well as their high percentage of fiber and immune booster vitamin C, bone-building vitamin K and manganese.

2 bananas
2 oranges
1 cup (155 g) frozen mixed berries
1 cup (237 ml) basic mylk (page 214)

Blend until it's all smooth. Sip and enjoy. *Ahhh.*

ALMOST A STRAWBERRY MYLKSHAKE

Like the name says, this is pretty dang close to a strawberry mylkshake (page 220) as far as flavor and color go. Make it, shake it, drank it.

2 bananas
1 orange
1 cup (149 g) frozen strawberries
2 cups (473 ml) basic mylk (page 214)

Blend. Slurp. *Mmm*. Feel free to garnish with whatever toppings you prefer, like cacao nibs, nuts or extra strawberries!

ALMOST A STRAWBERRY MYLKSHAKE … PLUS SPIRULINA!

In other words: all the same benefits, and it's green.

2 bananas
1 orange
1 cup (149 g) frozen strawberries
2 cups (473 ml) basic mylk (page 214)
1 tbsp (5 g) spirulina powder
1 tbsp (10 g) hemp seeds

Blend everything together until it's evenly dark green.

GREEN GINGER PEAR JOY

I made this recipe one morning for my partner before we set out on a day of adventuring; I could not have blended up a better start! It's sweet, flavorful and full of life. If you love spinach, pears and ginger—you will adore this smoothie.

Note: If you don't have frozen pear slices on hand, you can just use fresh pear and add a few ice cubes.

2 tbsp (29 g) ginger
2 oranges
2 pitted dates
2 cups (346 g) frozen pear slices
4 cups (120 g) spinach
2 cups (473 ml) water

Peel the ginger and oranges. Throw everything into the blender and whizz it up until smooth and bright green. Woo!

TROPIKALE ENERGIZER

With plenty of citrus, vitamin C, potassium, fiber and healthy carbs, this drink will give you energy for hours. This is typically what I make most mornings after yoga and man oh man it makes me feel sunny from the inside out (I mean that in a good way).

2 bananas
2 oranges
1 cup (165 g) frozen pineapple
1 cup (67 g) kale
2 pitted dates
2 cups (473 ml) water

Blend everything up until smooth and a vibrant green color. Sip in the sunshine!

MELLOW YELLOW

This is one of my fave recipes because it's sweet, simple and absolutely bursting with vitamin C. Drink this if you feel a cold coming on . . . or every day just because it tastes great and your body wants it!

1 cup (155 g) frozen mango
2 bananas
1 cup (165 g) pineapple
1 orange
1 cup (237 ml) basic mylk (page 214)

Blend all the ingredients until smooth and glowing yellow. Well . . . not literally glowing.

GINGER CILANTRO MANGO ELIXIR

This is both refreshing and cleansing. Ginger and cilantro are amazing for your blood, and they taste delicious paired with sweet tropical fruits like mango and banana.

1 cup (25 g) cilantro leaves
1 green apple, seeded
1 tbsp (15 g) ginger
1 cup (237 ml) water
½ cucumber
1 frozen banana
1 cup (155 g) frozen mango

Blend everything up until smooth and green. Drink it!

MACA BLUEBERRY BLESSING

One of my all-time favorites, this smoothie gives off all kinds of organic love vibes. It's vibrant in color, nutrients and taste! Maca and coconut water add extra benefits including electrolytes, making this recipe a great choice during exercise. I think I'm a blueberry addict. That's a legitimate condition, right?

1 cup (155 g) frozen blueberries
1 banana
2 oranges, seeded
1 tbsp (5 g) maca powder
2 cups (473 ml) coconut water

Blend everything up until smooth and beautifully purple. Enjoy.

CITRUS MANGO SAMBA

This smoothie is gonna make you wanna get up and shake your tail feather, especially if you're already listening to some good ole Mungo Jerry. The citrus adds a bit of tartness, but the sweetness from the mango balances it all out.

1 cup (155 g) frozen mango
1 grapefruit, seeded
1 lemon, seeded
1 orange
1 cup (237 ml) water

Blend everything together until smooth. Drink! Dance!

PINEAPPLE BERRY MIXER

I love pineapple in smoothies—it is super sweet and at the same time it gives you a little bit of tartness. You may not know this because it seems counterintuitive, but tart fruits like lemons and pineapple actually become alkalizing (not acidic) once they enter your system—huh! Alkalizing foods keep your blood healthy. Eat more of them.

1 cup (240 g) pineapple
⅓ cup (51 g) frozen blueberries
⅓ cup (51 g) frozen raspberries
⅓ cup (50 g) frozen mulberries
1 cup (237 ml) basic mylk (page 214)

Blend it all up until smooth and a vibrant deep purple. Enjoy.

MINT CACAO KISS

I called this one a kiss because it's light, sweet and you're probably going to fall in love with it, or at least share it with someone you also share kisses with. Peppermint is great for taming an upset tummy, and when the creamy green smoothie is paired with crunchy, bitter cacao nibs, you've got one cup of "Holy Delicious!"

1 cup (24 g) mint leaves
1 orange
2 frozen bananas
1 cup (237 ml) spiced mylk (page 217)
1 tbsp (11 g) cacao nibs

Blend everything together (except the cacao nibs) until smooth and green and top off with the nibs. *Crunch!*

VANILLA MELON MAGIC

The deliciousness of this recipe caught me off guard; I was expecting it to taste good, but it totally blew my mind beyond that! It's like a fruity vanilla mylkshake! Kids and adults alike will love this one.

1 cantaloupe (about 3 cups [531 g])
1 cup (155 g) frozen mango
1 tsp vanilla powder

Spoon out the fruit of the cantaloupe and put in a blender with the mango and vanilla—blend it all until smooth, creamy and thick. *Mmm!*

DRINK FOR BEAUTY

All the ingredients in this recipe do amazing things for your skin (it's your largest organ, by the way, so we gotta take care of it).

1 cup (155 g) frozen blueberries
1 cup (237 ml) coconut kefir
1 cup (245 g) almond yogurt
1 tbsp (28 g) lucuma powder
1 orange
1/16 tsp stevia powder

Blend everything together until smooth and creamy.

PIÑA COLADA

I'll have one straight up, thanks.

Note: Refrigerate the pineapple overnight before making this if you want it to be cold.

1 pineapple
¼ cup (60 ml) coconut milk (optional)

Cut off the skin, chop up the fruit and blend until smooth, adding the coconut milk if you're using it. Yep. That's it.

APPLES AND BANANAS

I like to eat 'em. Or in this case . . . drink 'em.

2 apples
2 frozen bananas
½ cup (120 g) spinach
1 cup (237 ml) basic mylk (page 214)

Remove the seeds from the apples and blend everything up until smooth.

MANGO COCONUT LASSI

This is an amazing drink. It is creamy, sweet and takes my mind to somewhere tropical and warm . . . I could probably drink this every day. Make it for Indian night!

2 cups (310 g) frozen mango
2 cups (490 g) coconut yogurt
1 cup (237 ml) coconut milk
1 tbsp (21 g) coconut nectar

Blend everything until smooth, thick and creamy. Enjoooooy.

HIP HIP HYDRATION

Although all the recipes in this book are great for keeping your body hydrated, the cucumber in this one goes the extra mile (or kilometer, since I'm Canadian).

1 cup (67 g) kale
1 cup (155 g) frozen mango
½ cucumber
1⁄16 tsp stevia powder
1-2 cups (237-473 ml) water

Blend everything until smooth, green and creamy!

LUCUMA LUXE

The color and flavor of this recipe seem very elegant, almost royal, to me. Make this smoothie and see if you agree.

1 cup (155 g) frozen berries
1 banana
1 mango
1 tbsp (28 g) lucuma powder
1 cup (237 ml) water

Blend all the ingredients until smooth.

YUMBERRY LOVE

Yumberries have historically been grown and enjoyed in China for a looong time, and with good reason. These berries have a uniquely sweet and tart taste, and provide huge amounts of polyphenols and anthocyanins; they are also known to help with liver function, skin complexion and eyesight.

1 cup (155 g) frozen mango
1 cup (240 g) pineapple
½ cucumber
1 tbsp (28 g) yumberry powder
1 cup (237 ml) water

Blend everything until smooth. Feel the love.

SEA BUCKTHORN SWEETNESS

Sea buckthorn grows in the deserts of Europe and Asia, where it must defend itself against the harsh climates, causing it to have countless antioxidants and bioactive components that are great for us!

2 bananas
2 oranges
6 ice cubes
1 tbsp (28 g) sea buckthorn powder

Blend it all up.

CHIA BUBBLE TEA

My friend, another Emily, gave me the idea for this recipe. I know people love bubble tea, so I made a healthy version.

½ cup (83 g) pineapple
1 cup (237 ml) basic mylk (page 214)
2 frozen bananas
1 orange
2 tbsp (16 g) chia seeds

Blend everything except the chia seeds until smooth and yellow. Pour the chia seeds into the bottom of a glass, then fill 'er on up with the smoothie.

PEPPERMINT CUCUMBER REFRESHER

My partner and I enjoyed this in a sunny backyard after a stressful day, and it calmed us both right down; I went from being extremely glum, sore and tired to feeling my best. Clearly, this drink has secret magical properties.

½ cucumber (you can leave the skin on if it's organic)
2 frozen bananas
½ cup (12 g) mint leaves
1 cup (165 g) pineapple
⅟₁₆ tsp stevia powder
2 cups (473 ml) water

Blend everything until smooth and green. *Ahhh.*

ANTI-INFLAMMATORY SMOOTHIE

After a tough workout, my muscles get sore. Cue . . . this recipe! All the ingredients are helpful with—you guessed it—relieving the discomfort of sore muscles and inflamed tissue.

1 cup (155 g) pitted cherries
1 cup (155 g) frozen blueberries
1 tbsp (15 g) ginger
2 oranges
1 cup (237 ml) water

Blend everything together until smooth and dark reddish/blue. Drink.

BOLD AND GOLD

More of a light yellow than gold, but I got your attention.

2 frozen bananas
3 apples, seeds removed
4 pineapple slices
2 cups (473 ml) water

Blend until smooth and gold (er . . . yellow-ish).

BLUEBERRYLICIOUS SMOOTHIE

I can't handle the deliciousness (let alone the berryliciousness).

1 cup (155 g) frozen blueberries
4 bananas
6 pitted dates
2 cups (473 ml) basic mylk (page 214)

Blend until smooth and creamy. *Mmm*, oh yes.

SWEET CHERRY ALMOND SMOOTHIE

This tastes even better than it sounds.

1 cup (155 g) frozen cherries
1 orange
1 cup (237 ml) basic mylk (page 214) made with almonds
3 pitted dates
1 banana

Blend it all up and slurp it down!

SMOOTHIE FOR YOUR SWEETHEART

I actually did make this one for my honeybun when we were on a juice and smoothie cleanse, and we both loved it.

2 bananas
2 apples, seeds removed
4 pineapple slices
½ cup (78 g) frozen berries
2 cups (473 ml) water

Blend until smooth and pink!

THE OGOPOGO

Supposedly in the Okanogan Valley, there is a lake where a mythical sea creature lives, and its folk name is Ogopogo (BC's very own Loch Ness Monster). The ingredients in this smoothie are symbols of the Okanogan's fertile soil and farms, and I look forward to seeing these iconic fruits every summer at farmers' markets.

2 peaches
1 cup (155 g) cherries, pitted
2 apples, seeds removed
1 cup (237 ml) basic mylk (page 214)

Blend everything up until smooth (make sure you pit the peaches!) and sip while contemplating what good ole Ogopogo is up to. . . .

chapter 5

SAVORY SMOOTHIES

The main ingredients in these recipes are non-sweet fruits (like cucumbers, tomatoes and bell peppers) and vegetables (like broccoli, carrots and onions). These foods are super low in calories while at the same time being amazingly micro- and macro-nutrient dense. For example, calorie for calorie, spinach has more protein than steak. Go plants! Popeye knew what was up.

Non-sweet fruits and vegetables are excellent foods for filling up on and getting a more than sufficient amount of vitamins, minerals and nutrients. This is because they contain enormous amounts of fiber, which give you the feeling of satiation. Many of these smoothie recipes also contain nuts and seeds for added nutritional benefits and to make the smoothie a legitimate meal.

If the idea of a savory smoothie is weird or unappealing to you, think of these recipes as soups; pour them in a bowl and top them off with chopped veggies and herbs. Ta-da! Healthy, flavorful bowls of fresh delight in just a few minutes. Or use these recipes as sauces: Pour them over brown rice and steamed veggies for an amazingly healthy and filling meal. The recipes in this chapter are great for lunch or dinner when you want to add in some extra, cleansing nutrition or when you simply don't feel like cooking. Just as sweet fruit smoothies are the perfect start to your day, savory veggie smoothies are the ideal meal when you're winding down.

Note: If ya wanna keep these recipes totally raw, skip the cooking part (except for the Creamy Onion and Potato Smoothie, page 209)! Simple. But keep in mind, it is creamier if you let the veggies simmer.

CREAMY BROCCOLI WITH GARLIC AND CILANTRO

This is a fantastic, flavorful green blend for lunch or dinner. I prefer to think of this recipe as creamy broccoli soup with garlic, herbs and spices. Enjoy it from a glass with a straw or in a bowl with a spoon! However it gets in you, it's gonna do good things.

2 cups (142 g) broccoli

1 clove garlic

2 tbsp (17 g) miso paste

1 orange

¼ cup (43 g) almonds

¼ cup (38 g) pitted dates

½ tsp coriander

½ tsp paprika

½ tsp turmeric

1 cup (16 g) cilantro

1 avocado (optional, but if you do use it remember to remove the pit)

1½ cups (355 ml) water, as needed

Peel, wash and chop everything as needed. Blend all the ingredients together, adding water as needed.

CURRIED CARROT CREAM

This is virtually fat-free and yet so creamy and flavorful! I like to think of it as carrot soup . . . I love eating it with a spoon and how it warms me right up with wholesome goodness. Try it for lunch or dinner.

5 large carrots
1 onion
3 cloves garlic
4 cups (946 ml) vegetable broth
Salt, pepper and curry powder, to taste

Wash, peel and chop the veggies and put them in a pot with the broth. Bring to a boil, then reduce to a simmer and keep it that way until the carrots are soft. Let the mixture cool down for about 30 to 60 minutes then blend until smooth and creamy, adding the salt, pepper and curry powder as desired. The taste is gonna blow your mind!

KINDA LIKE TOMATO SOUP SMOOTHIE

Obviously, I had trouble thinking of a name for this one. In any case, it's freaking delicious. My fave way to eat it? As a sauce with rice and veggies.

1 cup (160 g) cherry tomatoes
1 avocado
1 tbsp (17 g) miso paste
Cumin, coriander, Himalayan salt and pepper, to taste
1 cup (237 ml) water
1 clove garlic

Blend everything until smooth and light red or orange-y, adding spices as desired. Serve with extra chopped avocado and cherry tomatoes!

TOMATO GARLIC SMOOTHIE WITH ONIONS AND SPICES

This is a delightfully tangy, savory and flavorful recipe that is perfect for dinner when you don't feel like eating something heavy or making something complicated.

2 cups (322 g) tomatoes
1 clove garlic
⅛ cup (25 g) onion
1 red bell pepper, seeds removed
1 avocado
Pinch Himalayan salt
1 tsp cumin
1 tsp coriander
1–2 cups (237–473 ml) water or vegetable broth

Blend everything until smooth. Serve with cilantro if ya want.

THE BEST CORN AND CAULIFLOWER SMOOTHIE

I first created this recipe while doing a liquid cleanse with my partner and I remember it tasting beyond amazing—it totally hit the spot that night. Now my mouth is watering just thinking about it.

1 head cauliflower
2 cups (272 g) corn
6 field tomatoes
1 avocado
Juice from ½ lime
1 clove garlic
2 tbsp (33 g) miso paste
Cumin and coriander, to taste
Hot water, as needed

Steam the cauliflower and corn until tender (or leave it raw if that is important to you), then put everything in your blender. Blend until smooth, adding water in ½ cup (118 ml) amounts until you have your desired consistency. This makes a lot. It should taste amazing. If it doesn't, adjust according to taste until you like what you've got.

MEXICO-INSPIRED SMOOTHIE

I have a dear friend who owns an amazing restaurant in Mérida, Yucatan; he is the inspiration for this recipe, since he is always making me drool when he describes the abundance of fresh fruits and veggies they have there.

5 tomatoes
2 cups (272 g) corn
1 avocado
Juice from ½ lime
1 tsp coriander
Pepper, to taste
Vegetable broth, as needed

Blend everything until smooth, adding the veggie broth in ½ cup (118 ml) amounts until you have your desired consistency. If you'd like a warm smoothie/soup, heat the vegetable broth before you add it.

SPICY CARROT SMOOTHIE WITH BELL PEPPERS

Creamy, vibrant, carotene-packed bliss in a bowl.

4 cups (512 g) carrots
1 onion
2 orange bell peppers
3 small tomatoes
Cumin and coriander, to taste
1 tsp lemon juice
3 pitted dates
Vegetable broth or water, enough to cover veggies in a pot

Roughly chop all the veggies. Cover the carrots and onions with vegetable broth or water in a pot and bring to a boil. Reduce heat to low and let them cook for about 30 minutes or until tender. Throw all the ingredients (including the veggie broth mix) into a high-speed blender and blend until smooth and creamy, adding the spices as you like. Serve with tomato slices and cilantro if you want!

CREAMY ONION AND POTATO SMOOTHIE

I couldn't believe how fabulous this tasted the first time I whipped it up. This recipe is oil-free and salt-free but it is just as satisfying—if not more so, since it's so healthy—as your regular potato soup (which is usually laden with butter and salt)!

6 potatoes
1 onion
2 cloves garlic
Enough vegetable broth to cover the potatoes and onions
1 tsp coriander
1 tsp dill
1 tsp fresh parsley

Slice the veggies then cover with the broth and bring to a boil. Reduce to a simmer and let cook until tender, around 25 minutes. Put everything into your blender and blend until smooth. It is shockingly delicious! Add whatever else you like.

SPICY AVOCADO AVIATOR

So. Creamy.

1 avocado
½ cucumber (you can leave the skin on if it's organic)
1 tsp lime juice
1 cup (245 g) coconut yogurt
1 clove garlic
½ tsp Himalayan salt
½ tsp chili powder, to taste

Blend everything until smooth, adding the spice as desired! This is really tasty when you add chunks of mango.

chapter 6

MYLKS & MYLKSHAKES

Why the "y"? No, it's not because I'm illiterate. Actually, I intentionally spell "mylk" in this book without the conventional "i" because all the recipes are dairy-free! If you currently consume dairy, before you freak out and stick your nose at me and my lack-of-lactose ways, lemme say a few things. Have you ever thought about why you are drinking the milk of another species when you are far past needing even your own mother's milk? It don't make no sense. Cow milk is for baby cows! On a more positive note, these non-dairy mylks have all the stuff you want from their cow-sourced counterparts, but I'd argue they're even better because no one gets hurt (if you think dairy is a harmless industry, I suggest you watch a documentary called *Earthlings* and check out page 253). The following recipes have all the calcium, vitamins, minerals, protein and deliciousness of regular milk, without the antibiotics, unnatural sourcing, processing or freaky stabilizers or artificially added nutrients.

For all these mylk recipes, you can use nuts (like almonds, pecans and walnuts), seeds (such as pumpkin, hemp and sunflower) or coconut meat (dried or fresh). I recommend using raw nuts or seeds and soaking them in water for at least 6 hours so their vitamins and nutrients are more easily absorbed by your body. Then rinse them off with fresh water and you're ready to roll!

BASIC MYLK

Simple and delicious. Perfect for adding to smoothies, granola or oatmeal. Use any kind of nut or seed you like; examples are almonds, cashews, pumpkin seeds, sunflower seeds, hemp seeds, pecans and macadamias. You could even use coconut meat! The nut or seed you use in this recipe will determine the flavor of the mylk. If you like cashews, use cashews! If pecans are your fave, try making pecan mylk. There are endless possibilities. Personally, I love walnuts, and so walnut mylk is my top pick. Also, keep in mind that some nuts allow for creamier mylk than others; cashews, pine nuts and macadamias are the best for this because of their high healthy fat content.

MAKES: 4 CUPS (946 ML)

1 cup (100 g) raw nuts or seeds
3 cups (710 ml) water

Cover the nuts in water and let them soak for 6 hours. Discard the soak water and rinse the nuts with fresh water. Blend the soaked nuts with fresh water until smooth, frothy and white. Strain through a nut mylk bag or cheesecloth (or leave as is). Drink right away or store in the fridge in a sealable glass container for up to one week.

SPICED MYLK

This recipe is sweetened with dates and more flavorful than the basic one because it includes spices. Absolutely amazing on its own or added to other recipes! I could drink this all day.

MAKES: 4½ CUPS (1 L)

1 cup (125 g) raw nuts, seeds or coconut meat
3 cups (710 ml) water
1 tsp cinnamon powder
½ tsp nutmeg powder
1 tsp vanilla extract
Pinch of pink Himalayan crystal salt
3–5 pitted dates

Cover the nuts in water and let them soak for 6 hours, then rinse and discard the soak water. Blend the soaked nuts, seeds or fresh coconut meat with all the other ingredients until smooth, frothy and white. Strain through a nut mylk bag or cheesecloth (or leave as is). Store in the fridge in a sealable glass container for up to one week.

CHOCOLATE MYLK

Chocolate. Mylk. Need I say more?

MAKES: 4½ CUPS (1 L)

Follow the recipe for spiced mylk, adding 1–2 tablespoons (28–56 g) of cacao powder and, if you like, 1 tablespoon (28 g) of maca powder.

VANILLA MYLKSHAKE

Simple, sublime, sexy: Sip it up.

MAKES: 4½ CUPS (1 L)

3 frozen bananas
1 cup (237 ml) basic mylk (page 214)
1 tsp vanilla powder
1 tsp vanilla extract
Pinch of Himalayan crystal salt
2–5 pitted dates

Blend it all up until thick and smooth. Pour into fancy glasses and savor with a straw . . . *mmm.*

CHOCOLATE MYLKSHAKE

This is about as delicious and healthful as any mylkshake can possibly be; drink it up and feel gooood. No, seriously. I don't think you understand how amazing this is yet. Make it ASAP.

MAKES: 3 CUPS (710 ML)

3 frozen bananas
1 cup (237 ml) basic mylk (page 214)
1 tsp vanilla powder
1 tbsp (28 g) cacao powder
¼ tsp cinnamon powder
¼ tsp cayenne powder
Pinch of Himalayan crystal salt
2–5 pitted dates
Cacao nibs, for topping

Blend it all up until thick and smooth. Add some cacao nibs for a crunch.

STRAWBERRY MYLKSHAKE

Although my favorite kind of mylkshake is chocolate (I am a shamelessly self-confessed chocoholic), I'm always delightfully surprised by the fresh, fruity flavor of strawberry shakes. They make me think of sunny summers in the backyard.

MAKES: 5 CUPS (1.2 L)

3 frozen bananas
1 cup (237 ml) basic mylk (page 214)
1 tsp vanilla powder
Pinch of Himalayan crystal salt
2–5 pitted dates
1 cup (221 g) fresh or frozen strawberries, plus sliced strawberries for garnish

Blend it all up until thick and smooth. Garnish with sliced strawberries for extra color.

CREAMY ICED CHAI LATTE

Who needs a $7.00 fancy drink from the coffee shop when you can make your own healthy version in the comfort of your kitchen? Nobody I know.

1 cup (237 ml) strongly brewed chai tea
2 cups (473 ml) basic mylk (page 214)
1 tbsp (21 g) coconut nectar
1 cup (5 g) ice cubes

Let the tea cool down, then blend the tea, mylk and coconut nectar together and serve over ice. You could alternatively blend the ice into the drink, too.

chapter 7

ENERGY BARS & HEALTHY SNACKS

These recipes for energy bars are perfect for staying satisfied in between meals, at the gym, in school or at work, and even as nutritious desserts. They contain ingredients like nuts, seeds, oats, dried fruit and other superfoods—but they are put together in creative ways that might make you feel surprised at how delicious healthy food can be! Don't be afraid of the fat content in nuts and seeds; the fats in these foods are excellent for your body and also necessary for you to survive! Fats function in the body to transport molecules, protect nerves and help brain function. Just keep in mind that you don't need much; your recommended daily intake is about ¼ cup (31 g) of nuts or seeds. My recipes don't go over that if you follow the serving suggestions. Also, don't be afraid of the sugars in dried fruit! Again, your body wants them. I suggest pairing these recipes with a glass of lemon water to keep your system hydrated, alkaline and nourished.

The recipes for snacks in this chapter are healthy solutions to those midday munchies that tempt many of us to hit up the vending machine for a bag of chips. Well, I say: no more! Next time you're gonna be prepared with a big bag of crunchy Cheezy Garlic Kale Chips instead (page 246). Those vending machine folks will be staring longingly at your snack box while you happily munch away. Heh heh heeeh. . . .

THE POWER BAR

This recipe has got everything you need to stay energized—while you exercise, work, play or practice whatever other activities fill your life. No need to buy expensive, fancy energy bars at the store—make your own! They are more affordable, probably healthier and taste better!

MAKES: 8 BARS

⅓ cup (55 g) flax seeds, ground into flour
⅓ cup (27 g) rolled oats, ground into flour
¼ cup (16 g) pumpkin seeds
¼ cup (16 g) hemp seeds
1 cup (93 g) dried shredded coconut
1¼ cup (190 g) pitted dates
2 tbsp (30 ml) melted coconut oil
1 tsp vanilla extract

Put everything into your food processor and process until it all sticks together. If it remains too crumbly, add more dates or coconut oil, or even some fresh lemon juice. Press into a lined 9 x 5-inch (23 x 13-cm) loaf pan and set in the fridge for about 3 hours. Garnish with more coconut shreds and pumpkin seeds, if you like. Slice into bars and enjoy! These will keep for about a week, but I am sure they'll be gone before that.

SEXY SEED MEDLEY

This recipe has three different superfood seeds—hemp, pumpkin and chia—that are chock full of protein, fiber, healthy fats, B vitamins, iron, phosphorus and potassium. Know what all those do for ya? They give you energy and strength, which allow you to work hard, live long and feel good . . . that's sexy. ("Ah, NOW I get it!")

MAKES: 8 BARS

1 cup (99 g) pecans
⅓ cup (48 g) chia seeds
⅓ cup (48 g) hemp seeds
⅓ cup (39 g) pumpkin seeds
2 cups (304 g) pitted dates
1 tsp vanilla extract
Pinch of Himalayan salt

Process the pecans into rough flour in a food processor. Add the rest of the ingredients and process until it all begins to stick together. Press into a lined 9 x 9-inch (23 x 23-cm) baking pan and let set in the fridge overnight, then cut into bars. Spread on peanut butter, drizzle on dark chocolate or sprinkle with dried fruit, coconut or cacao nibs.

COCO OAT BARS WITH PEANUT BUTTER AND CAROB

These are a great snack to bring to work, school, traveling or elsewhere because they are easy to transport and provide deliciously wholesome energy quick. Think of them as healthy peanut butter chocolate bars.

MAKES: 6 BARS

BARS
1 cup (81 g) oats
½ cup (46 g) coconut shreds
⅓ cup (60 g) peanut butter
3 tbsp (45 ml) melted coconut oil
1 tsp vanilla extract
Pinch of Himalayan salt

DATE PASTE
1 cup (152 g) pitted dates
¼–½ cup (60–120 ml) water, as needed
pinch of Himalayan salt

CAROB COATING
1 tbsp (15 ml) melted coconut oil
1 tbsp (28 g) carob powder

Mix the bar ingredients together with a spoon until the oats are coated and you can press the mixture together. Press into the bottom of a lined baking pan and put in the fridge for an hour.

To make the date paste, blend everything together until smooth, adding water as needed to create a thick, creamy mixture. Alternatively, you can make date syrup and add water until you have a more liquid consistency.

Mix the carob coating ingredients and date paste together in a bowl. Then, spread the carob coating onto the bars, slice and enjoy!

PEPPERMINT SPIRULINA BARS WITH CHOCOLATE FUDGE

These are full of protein and fiber—great for after a run. If you have thyroid issues or are pregnant, consult your doctor before consuming maca.

MAKES: 16 BARS

CRUST
1 cup (81 g) oats
1 cup (152 g) pitted dates
1 tsp vanilla extract

PEPPERMINT SPIRULINA LAYER
1 cup (111 g) cashews
1 cup (152 g) pitted dates
3–4 tbsp (84–112 g) spirulina powder
2 tbsp (30 ml) melted coconut oil
⅛ cup (3 g) packed mint leaves

Pinch of Himalayan salt
1 cup (237 ml) water, as needed

CHOCOLATE FUDGE
1 cup (152 g) pitted dates
1 cup (237 ml) water
2 tbsp (14 g) cacao powder
1 tbsp (7 g) maca powder
Cacao nibs and pumpkin seeds

To make the crust, pulse the oats into a powder in a food processor and add the dates and vanilla, processing until it all begins to stick together. Press into the bottom of a lined bread pan. Put in the fridge for 30 minutes so it hardens.

To make the peppermint spirulina layer, blend all the ingredients until smooth, adding as little water as possible. Spread onto your crust and put in the freezer until solid (about 2 hours).

To make the chocolate fudge, blend all the ingredients until smooth and thick. Spread onto your peppermint spirulina layer and leave in the fridge for 24 to 48 hours. Top with cacao nibs and pumpkin seeds, and slice.

DARK CHOCOLATE CHIP, OAT AND HEMP COOKIES

These could alternatively be called "OMG Cookies" because that was my immediate response to tasting them. Better than any baked cookie I've ever had, these dark chocolate chip, oat and hemp cookies only contain healthful, whole foods that make you feel and look fabulous.

MAKES: 10 HUGE COOKIES OR 20 NORMAL ONES

CHOCOLATE
2 tbsp (42 g) cacao powder
2 tbsp (30 ml) melted coconut oil
1 tbsp (21 g) coconut nectar

COOKIES
2 cups (222 g) cashews
¾ cup (108 g) hemp seeds
1 cup (81 g) oats
¼ cup (85 g) coconut nectar
¼ cup (60 ml) melted coconut oil
Pinch of Himalayan salt
1 tsp vanilla extract

To make the chocolate, whisk all the ingredients together until smooth. Pour into the bottom of a pan or on a plate and put in the freezer for 20 minutes or until solid, then cut or break apart into chocolate chip-size pieces.

To make the cookies, pulse the cashews and hemp seeds into powder in a food processor then add the rest of the ingredients and process until it all sticks together. Break up in a large bowl, then add the chocolate chips and mix everything together with your hands. Roll into cookies, or use an ice cream scoop. Drizzle with more chocolate, if desired.

GREEN EARTH ORBS

These orbs have a delicious, deep nutty flavor and are positively packed with healthy nuts and seeds that will make your skin glow and your body sing!

MAKES: 15 ORBS

1 cup (31 g) walnuts
1 cup (64 g) pumpkin seeds
½ cup (72 g) chia seeds
1 cup (152 g) pitted dates
2 tbsp (27 g) coconut oil
¼ tsp Himalayan salt
1 tsp cinnamon

Pulse the nuts and seeds into powder in a food processor, then add the rest of the ingredients and process until it all begins to stick together. Try rolling a small handful into a ball. If it works, roll the rest of the mixture into balls. If it is still too crumbly, add more coconut oil or dates. Roll the balls in coconut and cinnamon for extra flavor and nutrition.

DARE TO DATE SQUARES

These squares are an excellent energy bar because they're mostly made up of dates and oats, both of which are full of healthy carbs (both simple and complex) that will keep you focused and full for hours! Combine these with fruit for an amazing breakfast, have them on their own for a delicious and quick snack or eat them as a super healthy dessert! Life is good when you've got a date (or several).

MAKES: 16 SQUARES

BASE
1 cup (81 g) rolled oats
1 cup (110 g) pecans
1 cup (152 g) pitted dates
1 tsp vanilla extract

MIDDLE
1½ cups (228 g) pitted dates
¼ cup (60 ml) melted coconut oil

¼ tsp Himalayan salt
½ cup (120 ml) water, as needed

TOPPING
¼ cup (20 g) rolled oats
¼ cup (28 g) pecans
1 tbsp (15 ml) melted coconut oil
Pinch Himalayan salt

To make the base, process the oats and pecans into flour in a food processor, then add the rest of the ingredients and process until it begins to stick together. Press into the bottom of a lined baking pan and put in the fridge.

To make the middle, put all the ingredients in your food processor and blend until smooth, adding water as needed in 1 tablespoon (15 ml) amounts to make it creamy, but keeping it thick enough so that it holds its shape. Spread evenly onto your base and put back in the fridge for about 30 minutes.

To make the topping, pulse all the ingredients in your food processor until they become a crumble-like consistency. Sprinkle evenly on top of the middle layer and press down lightly. Let the recipe sit in the fridge overnight so it can set and develop more flavor. Slice and enjoy!

ONION ROSEMARY FLAX BREAD

A cross between bread and crackers, this recipe is super nutritious and full of fiber to keep you nourished and satisfied. Enjoy it with hummus, nut pâté or pesto and layer with veggies for a delicious meal, or nibble it naked for a healthy snack. My fave way to eat this? With some kale olive tapenade, cucumber and tomato slices. Oh—and you gotta add avocado. Always avocado. Forever avocado.

MAKES: 12 SLICES

1¼ cup (180 g) flax seeds
½ cup (76 g) onion
1 yellow bell pepper
1 tbsp (2 g) dried rosemary
1 tsp coriander
Salt and pepper, to taste

Grind 1 cup (144 g) of the flax seeds into flour in your blender. Combine with all the other ingredients, as well as the remaining flax, in a food processor and process until it becomes like a thick paste. Spread evenly into a 0.1–0.2-inch (0.25–0.5-cm)-thick square on a dehydrator tray. Dehydrate for 1 to 2 hours then cut into squares and flip them over. Dehydrate for another 1 to 2 hours until pliable. Alternatively, you can use your oven at its lowest temperature, for about the same amount of time.

HIPPIE HEMP HUMMUS

Made with hemp seed butter instead of the traditional sesame seed butter,
I dare say I prefer this version to the original! I had trouble stopping myself from
devouring the entire bowl before I photographed it. This tastes phenomenal
with carrots, cucumber, celery and sun-dried tomatoes . . . and pretty much
everything else.

MAKES: 3½ CUPS (793 G)

2 cups (304 g) cooked chickpeas
1 cup (250 g) hemp seed butter
¼ cup (54 g) extra virgin olive oil
1 tsp Himalayan salt
2 cloves garlic
½ tsp coriander
Juice from 1 lemon
Water, as needed

Put everything in the food processor and pulse until it becomes smooth (like hummus),
adding water as needed in 1 tablespoon (15 ml) amounts to get the desired consistency.
Adjust according to taste and then enjoy with fresh veggies!

CH-CH-CH-CHIA PUDDING

The base of this recipe is chia seeds. That's right, the same plant that grows the grass for Ch-ch-ch-chia Pets is also one of the most nutritionally dense foods on the planet. I'll never get over that.

MAKES: 1¼ CUPS (345 G)

1 cup (237 ml) basic mylk (page 214)
1 tbsp (9 g) raisins
½ tsp vanilla powder
½ tsp cinnamon
3 tbsp (27 g) chia seeds
Fresh mint, for topping
Cacao nibs, for topping

Blend everything but the chia seeds until smooth, stir in the seeds and wait a few minutes for them to gel. Enjoy! I like this served with fresh mint and cacao nibs.

CHEEZY GARLIC KALE CHIPS

I bet you can't eat just one.

MAKES: 4 CUPS (230 G)

2–3 bunches kale
1 cup (111 g) cashews
2 tbsp (19 g) nutritional yeast
Juice from 1 lemon
1 tbsp (17 g) miso paste
1 red bell pepper
1 tomato
1 clove garlic

Take the stems off the kale, then tear the leaves into large pieces (ideally the size of your palm); set aside the leaves in a large bowl. Blend the rest of the ingredients until smooth and the consistency of thick sauce. Work the sauce into the kale leaves with your hands, massaging the leaves as you go until every one is coated. Throw in the oven at its lowest temperature, or your dehydrator, for 2 to 3 hours or until the kale leaves become crunchy. Personally, I like them best before they get crunchy, so I suggest you taste-test at all stages!

RESOURCES

Read this chapter first! It has all the info you want and need that will help you learn your way around the kitchen as well as a new, healthier lifestyle! I've got a section that focuses on equipment, where I recommend what brands of juicers, blenders and food processors are best suited to you. I have a section on techniques, in which I explain some tips and tricks for easy juicing, blending and wholesome eating. I have a section that elaborates on some of the less common (but super awesome) ingredients I will be occasionally using in my recipes. Last, but certainly not least, I have created a section that includes lists of important books, documentaries and websites that have guided me on my own journey to long-term wellness, compassion and happiness. I think they might just change your life.

EQUIPMENT

Guess what? To make juice, you need a juicer. To make smoothies, you need a blender. Shocked? Yeah, I thought so (please note the sarcasm that those words were soaked in). If you don't want to spend a whack load of money, you don't have to be biting off your nails right now—there are very affordable options available. That being said, with increased price comes increased quality. The best juicers and blenders are an investment, but they are also well worth their cost. I suggest evaluating how serious of a juicer/smoothie drinker you are. How often do you drink or want to drink juice and smoothies? How often do you have time to? What is your budget? If you're just beginning your experimentation with this, start out with a less expensive piece of equipment and see if you are happy with it, or if eventually you want more. Tip: Before you buy a juicer, you can try using a blender to make juice. Blend up the ingredients for the juice recipe then strain them through cheesecloth or a sieve. Personally I think this should be used only as a temporary method because it's not as efficient; you lose a large amount of potential juice, but it works as a trial method. You can find all these pieces of equipment online (at Amazon.com, for example) very easily, or check out your local health food store and you might get lucky!

JUICERS

ENTRY-LEVEL: Hamilton Beach Big Mouth Juicer ($60.00).

MID-RANGE: Breville JE98XL ($145.00). I haven't used it myself, but a lot of people swear by it.

BEST: Hurom HP Slow Juicer ($379). It does it all, and it does it well. You can pump all kinds of fruits, veggies and greens into this baby every day and it never complains. Other excellent brands are Green Star and Champion.

BLENDERS

ENTRY-LEVEL: Hamilton Beach Mid-Wave Crusher Blender ($53).

MID-RANGE: Nutri Ninja Blender ($100).

BEST: Vitamix 5200 ($400). It's the king of blenders (or queen, if we're into gender equality, and we are). Blendtec is on the same level, but I have my personal preference for Vitamix because it's all I've ever used, and I'd marry mine if I could.

FOOD PROCESSORS

You don't need one to make juice or smoothies, but in the Energy Bars & Healthy Snacks chapter (page 225) some recipes ask for a food processor. You can find them from anywhere between $50.00 to $200.00. I recommend Cuisinart or KitchenAid models. I use mine every single day to make everything from banana chocolate pudding to chili peanut sauce, so it's definitely a useful tool to have in the kitchen.

MYLK BAGS

If you haven't gotten to the chapter on mylks and mylkshakes yet, you're probably wondering what the heck I am talking about (and rightly so . . . a "mylk bag" sounds extremely strange and slightly freaky). Read page 213 first, then you'll dig me. These bags are used to squeeze out creamy mylk after you blend up nuts, seeds or coconut with water. You can alternatively use a cheesecloth or a simple sieve, but I believe in using the right tool for the job . . . so spend $25.00 and get outfitted properly.

TECHNIQUES
JUICING

For quicker juice making, prepare your produce as soon as you buy it (if you know how often you make juice). Wash, peel and chop the produce as needed, then store in glassware in the fridge. If you have favorite juice recipes that you make frequently, put all the ingredients in one container, and make several containers (for example, make seven at the beginning of each week for speedy juice every day).

While using the juicer, alternate between juicing juicy fruits and harder vegetables and leafy greens (for example, switch between pieces of apple with kale leaves). This keeps everything lubricated and moving. Did that sound naughty? A little bit.

To get your juice ultra-smooth, I suggest straining it after it's been through your juicer. The machine will have already strained it to some degree but doing it a second time takes it to the next level. Yes, you will have next-level juice. This is a personal preference, though, and my mom actually likes her juice without any extra straining. To each their own.

If you are a busy beaver (or human) and don't have time to make juice every day or more than once each day—you can still have juice that often! Make it in batches that will last up to two days. I wish I could say make juice for a week in one day but honestly, it's only nutritionally worth drinking within 48 hours since it oxidizes very fast. Ideally, you should be drinking your juice within 20 minutes but hey—life isn't fair, and we need to work with the schedules we each have. Store your juice in airtight glassware and keep in the fridge.

BLENDING

Like with juicing, if you know how often you will be making a particular smoothie recipe, prep your produce as soon as you bring it home and keep it in appropriate containers in the fridge.

To make really creamy, refreshingly cold smoothies, it's a good idea to have a fraction of the ingredients be frozen; frozen bananas or berries are my favorites to use, but any fruits or veggies will do . . . even dark leafy greens. I often add frozen kale or Swiss chard to my smoothies, and you can buy frozen spinach from most grocery stores. If frozen fruits or veggies aren't handy, just throw in a few ice cubes, but keep in mind this waters the smoothie down, so make sure to add a little less liquid, too.

This may seem obvious, but if your smoothie is too thick, add more liquid. If it's too thin, add more solids or superfood powders. I personally like mine pretty thin so I add 2 to 3 cups (473 to 710 ml) of liquid to my smoothies. If it tastes too watery, add a few dates or a tablespoon (7 g) of your fave superfood powder.

NOTE: I choose to buy mostly organic, so I prefer leaving the skin of my fruits and veggies intact (e.g., apples, cucumber, beets, carrots). When I buy non-organic produce, I peel most of it. We don't want pesticides in our juice! Ain't nobody got time for that. I understand that organic produce can cost much more than the conventionally grown stuff, but if you can afford it, choosing to support and eat organically grown food is very important. It will positively impact your long-term health, the well-being of the planet and the local farmers who are doing honest work (not greedy mega-sized agribusiness corporations)!

INGREDIENTS

I sometimes use uncommon ingredients in my recipes. They're all incredibly powerful foods, but you may not have heard of them until now. Let's change that! I wanna give you a brief description of them, as well as explain why they're so darn good for ya. Many of these foods have been used to heal the body for thousands of years in cultures across the globe; they are the original tried-and-true players. You should be able to find the following ingredients in your local health food store or grocery store that has a selection of health food products. Alternatively, you can buy online (I recommend Upaya Naturals if you're in Canada).

- DATES: I think most folks have heard of dates, and you may even have tried them before. They're a dried fruit that comes from the date palm, originating around the Persian Gulf, and have been cultivated since forever ago (no, really—we've been eating dates for so long we can't even remember when we started). They are sweet, gooey, delicious bites of fudge in my opinion. I recommend using Medjool dates because they are the largest and have a unique caramel-like flavor, but any kind will work for my recipes. Always remember to take the pits out!

- CACAO: Cacao powder comes from the cacao bean and is an ancient superfood, originally consumed by the Mayan civilization to give them strength and mental focus. Basically, cacao is raw chocolate. It has amazing amounts of fiber, zinc and iron. It is also an aphrodisiac . . . *mmmhmmm* . . . If you can't find cacao powder, you can use cocoa powder instead.

- MACA: Maca powder is another superfood that comes from a root that grows in the mountains of Peru. It has hormone-balancing properties and plenty of B vitamins and calcium. The flavor is pretty unique; it reminds me of molasses.

- SPIRULINA: This dark green powder is derived from algae and has impressive amounts of protein, essential amino acids and iron. You can tell by the deep, rich color that this food also provides a great dose of chlorophyll, which acts as a blood cleanser and takes part in many other essential functions.

- HEMP SEEDS: These little guys have a delicious nutty flavor and provide the perfect ratio of omega 3s and 6s, which work to improve brain function and play a role in metabolism. Hemp is an amazing food that can save the world! It's very energy-efficient to grow, and we can use it for everything from clothing to rope to paper . . . to food!

- FLAX SEEDS: Cultivated as early as 3000 BCE in Babylon, flax is a seed composed mostly of healthy fats—omega 3s—and fiber. It also provides great amounts of B vitamins, manganese and phytochemicals. Studies have shown it may help fight against heart disease, diabetes and cancer.

- COCONUT WATER: Coming from inside fresh young coconuts, coconut water is a super hydrating liquid filled with electrolytes and naturally filtered through the flesh of the coconut to give you pure refreshment. Buy your own coconuts and crack them open to get the water inside, or look for bottled 100 percent pure organic coconut water in the store.

- LUCUMA: This powder is derived from a fruit (coming from Andean valleys in Peru) and is popularly used to flavor ice cream because of its sweetly tart and fruity profile. It provides substantial amounts of carotene and several B vitamins.

- COCONUT NECTAR: I use this as a natural sweetener in a few of my recipes. Think of coconut nectar as a healthier maple syrup; it comes from coconut palms and undergoes minimal processing, which allows all the nutrients (including amino acids, B vitamins, vitamin C and minerals) to stay alive so you can benefit from them. If you can't find coconut nectar, you can use maple syrup instead.

- STEVIA: This white powder comes from the stevia plant and is one potent sweetener! It is calorie-free because the sweetness doesn't come from carbohydrates; instead it's simply the flavor of the plant's leaves. Use it very sparingly: only $\frac{1}{16}$ of a teaspoon or less per single serving. You can also find stevia in liquid form, and in that case, just a few drops are needed.

- HIMALAYAN SALT: This is a mineral-rich salt that is mined in Pakistan, and I like to use it in very small amounts to enhance the flavor of some of my recipes. It's always optional if you prefer to keep recipes salt-free.

- COCONUT OIL: I only use virgin, cold-pressed, organic coconut oil, and I recommend you do the same if you wish to get all its wonderful health benefits. Coconut oil is composed of medium chain triglycerides that can have therapeutic effects on the brain because of how they are metabolized, as well as increase your metabolism, which can lead to weight loss (if you need it)! Once digested, coconut oil has anti-bacterial, anti-fungal and anti-viral properties. I love using coconut oil on my skin as an all-natural moisturizer and sunscreen, too. If you are allergic to or can't find coconut oil, you can use cacao butter or cocoa butter instead.

BOOKS, DOCUMENTARIES & WEBSITES

These books, documentaries and websites have all helped me learn about healthy eating and living over the past few years. I think they will prove very useful to you as well. In my opinion, to succeed at anything (including long-term wellness) you need to be educated and informed about it.

BOOKS

- *The China Study* by T. Colin Campbell and Thomas Campbell
- *Diet for a New America* by John Robbins
- *The Food Revolution* by John Robbins and Dean Ornish M.D.
- *Eat To Live* by Joel Fuhrman
- *Breaking the Food Seduction* by Neal D. Barnard
- *Raw and Beyond* by Victoria Boutenko, Elaina Love and Chad Sarno
- *Eating Animals* by Jonathan Safran Foer
- *Fast Food Nation* by Eric Schlosser
- *The Way We Eat* by Peter Singer
- *The Face On Your Plate* by Jeffrey Moussaieff Masson
- *Mad Cowboy* by Howard F. Lyman
- *The Thrive Diet* by Brendan Brazier
- *The Omnivore's Dilemma* by Michael Pollan
- *In Defense of Food* by Michael Pollan
- *Prevent and Reverse Heart Disease* by Caldwell Esselstyn
- *Becoming Vegetarian* by Brenda Davis and Vesanto Melina
- *Becoming Vegan* by Brenda Davis and Vesanto Melina
- *Becoming Raw* by Brenda Davis and Vesanto Melina

DOCUMENTARIES

- *Earthlings*
- *Making the Connection*
- *Queen of the Sun*
- *Forks Over Knives*
- *Zeitgeist* (series)
- *Food, Inc.*
- *The Corporation*
- *Flow*
- *Super Juice Me!*
- *King Corn*
- *Vegucated*
- *Fat, Sick & Nearly Dead*
- *Simply Raw: Reversing Diabetes in 30 Days*
- *Food Matters*
- *Hungry For Change*
- *The Future of Food*
- *Sweet Misery*
- *The 11th Hour*

WEBSITES

- Finding Vegan
- One Green Planet
- Renegade Health
- Natural News
- World Society for the Protection of Animals
- ForestEthics
- Happy Cow
- Vegan Bodybuilding & Fitness
- VegSource
- Fitness Blender
- Happy Healthy Vegan
- ADAPTT (Animals Deserve Absolute Protection Today and Tomorrow)

ACKNOWLEDGMENTS

Thanks to Page Street Publishing for asking me to write another book! I never wanna stop!

Thank you, Mum and Daddy, for your constant support, encouragement and confidence in me. You're my number one fan, Mom!

Dan and Greg: I am grateful for your tolerance of my weird ways.

To all my taste-testing friends, thanks for your seemingly bottomless stomachs and endless words of love.

Hugs and kisses to every single person who has read and/or recommended my blog; you've brought me here and I'll never forget it! I'm on my knees in thanks (literally, I am sitting on the floor right now).

Lastly and definitely not least, I have to thank you. Even if you don't know me, I can confidently say I think you're a beautiful, unique individual and I love you . . . for real.

ABOUT THE AUTHOR

EMILY VON EUW (pronouns: they/them/theirs) is the creator of the award-winning recipe blog This Rawsome Vegan Life (thisrawsomeveganlife.com) and bestselling author of multiple cookbooks, including the bestselling *Rawsome Vegan Baking*. Em's passion in life comes from friendships, food, wilderness, mindfulness, lots of dark chocolate and this magical present moment! Emily has presented at veg expos and festivals across Canada and the US, and their work has been featured in publications around the world. Em lives with their wonderful girlfriend on Vancouver Island, Canada, on land belonging to the Snuneymuxw First Nation.

thisrawsomeveganlife.com
@thisrawsomeveganlife
@emilyvoneuw
@rawsomevegan

INDEX